Is There More?

Is There More?

Heaven, Hell, and the Eternal Life that Begins Now

Leslie D. Weatherhead

Abingdon Press

Nashville

Is There More?
Heaven, Hell, and the Eternal Life That Begins Now

Originally published as Life Begins at Death,
Copyright © 1969 by Denholm House Press
Festival paperback edition published by
Abingdon Press 1981
New edition copyright © 2011 by Abingdon Press

ISBN-13: 978-1-4267-4358-0

All Scripture quotations are from the King James Version of the Bible.

11 12 13 14 15 16 17 18 19 20—10 9 8 7 6 5 4 3 2 1
MANUFACTURED IN THE UNITED STATES OF AMERICA

Contents

Publisher's Preface

While questions about life beyond death are always with us, sometimes they become especially urgent. Realizing that we are living in just such a moment, Abingdon Press has decided to re-release a classic volume on this subject by Leslie D. Weatherhead, whose book *The Will of God* has helped millions of readers better understand God's will for their life. In this book, originally published as *Life Begins at Death*, Dr. Weatherhead answers such questions as whether we will reunite with loved ones in heaven, whether all chance of returning to God ends with the death of the body, what are the best ways to prepare ourselves for an eternity spent with God, and the like.

The book began as a recorded question-and-answer session between Dr. Weatherhead and his friend Norman French (Mr. French's questions appear in italics). For this new edition, the publisher has updated some of the language of the book and has deleted a small number of references to persons or events that were familiar to the book's original audience, but might not be as recognizable to today's readers.

Foreword

Is there life after death? Some believe there is, many say they don't know, and the remainder believe death is the end of our existence. Predictably, among those who have no association with any church, nine out of ten either don't believe in life after death or would class themselves as "don't knows." What is more surprising is that the same is true of more than a third of those who do profess a link with one denomination or another—though probably that link is, in many cases, nominal.

It is clear that many people are uncertain about a belief that has been held by the Christian church ever since the Resurrection of Jesus Christ. But even those who do believe have questions they would dearly like answered.

This brief book seeks to respond to those questions. Does our life continue after we die? If so, what is the evidence? And what do we know about the nature of the afterlife? Will it give us a chance to make good our shortcomings and the failures of this present life? Is reincarnation to be rejected out-of-hand, or might there be something in it? These are but a few of the questions raised.

Humanity's supposed survival of death is a fascinating subject and rarely dealt with from the pulpit, partly because there is so little in the Bible to go on. Yet we speculate and wonder and question. I hope you will find help in the answers given here.

Leslie D. Weatherhead
Bexhill-on-Sea

Though I am dead, grieve not for me with tears,
Think not of death with sorrowing and fears,
I am so near that every tear you shed
Touches and tortures me, though you think me dead
But when you laugh and sing in glad delight,
My soul is lifted upward to the Light:
Laugh and be glad for all that Life is giving,
And I though dead will share your joy in
living.

—Source Unknown

CHAPTER 1

Some Fundamentals

Dr. Weatherhead, why do Christians believe in life after death?

Because, first, they accept the teaching of Christ. After all, on the cross he said to a dying revolutionary, "Today thou shalt be with me in paradise" (Luke 23:43). Those who are dying don't bluff one another. Please notice that Jesus did not say, "I *hope* we shall meet again; I have faith that we may live after this life." His words, which are recorded only by Luke the doctor, have a tremendous ring of certainty about them. Not "I hope" or "I believe," but "Today thou shalt be with me in paradise." And he says to his Father, "Father, into thy hands I commend my spirit" (Luke 23:46). Those are not the words of a man whose personality is being obliterated by death. So if Christians accept the teaching of their Master, I think they are bound to accept that there is such a thing as life after death.

The second reason is that they feel another life is necessary to make sense of this one. To thousands of people this life seems to have no purpose or meaning, no overriding direction, whatsoever. Many have never really lived, in our sense. They have been handicapped in one way or another; indeed, none of us will die feeling we have exhausted our possibilities. Therefore many people feel that unless there's another life, this one is purposeless and all but meaningless. Another life is needed to make sense of this one.

Then another point to remember is that indubitably Christ himself rose from the dead. If the crucifixion had been the end of Christ it would have been the end of his religion. However we explain the *manner* of the resurrection, to me it is clear beyond all possibility of doubt that the *essential* Christ survived death and proved his survival to his followers. That made them feel that there must be a life beyond and different from life in the physical body.

For those reasons Christians believe in life after death.

But Christ was unique, and because he survived death this does not necessarily mean that we will all survive death, does it?

I quite agree. We can't say that because something happens to a unique person it will necessarily happen to other persons. But it does prove that there is such a thing as life that is different from, and on another plane than, life in a physical body. Also Jesus is reported as assuring the thief, "I shall meet you again." The Fourth Gospel reports him as saying, "I go to prepare a place for you" (John 14:2). I think survival is inherent in the nature of our personality, so I am not arguing that because he rose from the dead, we shall rise in the same way. Clearly we do not do so. He left an empty tomb. We do not. But for the reasons given, the evidence strongly is that we do survive and that his resurrection proves that there is another plane of being on which people live.

Would you say that unless one did believe in life after death, one could not rightly call oneself a Christian?

I am very hesitant to say about any credal statement, "Unless you believe this you are no Christian." I would define a Christian as a person who tries to interpret life—or who tries to face life's demands and challenges—in Christ's spirit and live according to Christ's will as far as he can discern it. I would regard the disciples as Christian even before Jesus died. Clearly the resurrection tremendously reinforced their faith in him and gave birth to the church, which has spread throughout the world. But if someone came to me and said, "I want to be a Christian but I am not sure about the resurrection," I would not deny him the title "Christian." I would say, "Try to live in his spirit, examine the evidence, listen to the testimony of the saints and missionaries and martyrs." And I would hope that he would come to accept survival, Christ's survival and our own, in that way. I would not like to exclude him from the very beginning from the title "Christian" because he did not possess this particular belief.

Jesus says very little about life after death. In fact the whole Bible tells us very little about it. Why is this?

It seems to me that Jesus was reticent for various reasons. One is that if life after death is so amazing and we knew details of it, we might be tempted to go into it by our own act before we had usefully finished life on this plane. Another is that we just haven't the capacity to understand what it is like. You can't explain what a sunset is like to a man who is born blind and remains blind. You can say, "It's gorgeous, it's scarlet, it's crimson, it's golden," but the words have no meaning. In the next life we shall probably have capacities for entering into a completely different form of life. We shall be on a different plane, with different dimensions and greater ranges of perception.

Perhaps this illustrates what I mean. When I was a young minister I had a dear friend, an Airedale dog, with which I used to go for walks. If I patted my knee and said, "Walk, boy, walk," he would wag his tail, jump up, bark, and be excited, because he knew what going for a walk meant. If I had said to him, "Now boy, we will go out and sit and enjoy the sunset," he would have expressed nothing but boredom and disappointment. In the same way, I feel that if Christ had tried to explain the next world, it would have been rather like my talking to my dog about sunsets. When Jesus talks about things that are on my plane, I can understand them and enter into them; but, to quote him, there are "yet many things to say to you, but you cannot bear them now. You can't understand them, you can't appreciate and enter into them." I feel that this may explain his reticence.

He also said things like, "In my Father's house are many mansions: if it were not so, I would have told you" (John 14:2).

Yes, that's a hint, isn't it? The word "mansions" has been much discussed by scholars. I follow Archbishop Temple in his interpretation of the word as meaning "inns at the side of the road." You remember the film The Inn of the Seventh Happiness? I remember preaching at the City Temple a sermon I called "Inns of Increasing Happiness." I think the act of dying means that you are, as it were, at the first inn at the side of the road. You rest there for a time, and you meet your dear ones. But then you "wake up in the morning," and you find that there is a road stretching on beyond you, and that there are more inns at the side of the road. Then you progress into deeper appreciation of human fellowship, but with also a deepening appreciation of divine fellowship, as you move along that road.

If I understand you correctly, you say there is no death. We live again. Why do we then have to die? Why can't we just go on living here?

First, I would not say there is no such thing as death. Death is a fact, and it was a fact of life before humanity appeared on the planet. The idea of death as the result of sin—which seems to haunt St. Paul—is, I think, erroneous. You ask why there must be such a thing as death. The physical body wears out, or it suffers from disease. It cannot, after a certain period, be the home of the spirit. It seems to me that death is essential, as birth is essential. One marks the beginnng of a period in which we inhabit a physical body, and the other marks the end of our inhabiting a physical body. But I believe that one's spirit existed before birth and continues after death. The physical life, including death, is only an incident. So you see that death is not nearly so important as we suppose. It is as unimportant as a milestone.

Yes, but I think there is a difficulty here. When I asked, "Since there is no such thing as death, why do we have to die?" you then declared that there is such a thing as death. But I have heard you use phrases like "the so-called death."

7

Death is certainly a fact, but it is rather a milestone on the road, or perhaps better still, embarking for another country, rather than ceasing to be. That is why I may speak of so-called death—to avoid the suggestion that it is the end of everything.

At death, do you mean that we simply discard this body? But what then survives? What is there of us that lives?

The essential personality, which expresses itself in some other form. You can call it an "etheric" body. The theory is that all the time we are in this body we are weaving some other kind of body— the etheric body as some people call it—in which we can manifest ourselves to our loved ones after death. And Jesus appears to have done that. He appeared to his beloved disciples, one Gospel says, "in another form." But they recognized him and he recognized them. Paul, you remember, spoke of a "spiritual body" (1 Corinthians 15:42-44).

Yet God gave us a terrific instinct of self-preservation. Why are we all afraid to die?

Well, not everyone is afraid to die. I'm not afraid to die. I have lived longer than you and therefore have gotten more out of life. I do rather dread the interim period between my present health and my death—the period when one might be ill and useless, a burden to oneself and others. But the idea of dying, taken by itself, is attractive to me. To wake up among old friends with a new body that doesn't hurt anywhere and is not worn out is most attractive.

But sometimes when I am driving you in my car you are extremely nervous. Now this must be because you are afraid of a car crash. This implies that you are afraid to die.

No. I am afraid of *suffering*. Actually I am not afraid when you drive, but I am very much afraid when some other friends of mine drive. If a crash killed me at once I shouldn't mind. But to lie in the hospital for ten weeks because the driver did not notice the light had turned red is enough to fill me with fear. Indeed, I think that kind of fear is a God-given thing.

No, I am not afraid of dying. I am afraid of the suffering that may lie between my present healthy state and death. I think death is an adventure, a gateway into a new life, in which you have further powers, deeper joys, and wonderful horizons.

I still want to press the question: Why then do we have to cling so ardently to this life? Why can't we just go ahead and rush into the next if it is going to be that much lovelier than here?

Because this life has something to teach us. As I see it, it is one of the lower grades in God's school, and you have to pass through it and you have to pass the exams at the end of it to graduate into the next. If you were so eager to leave this life that you took your own life when you might have served others and learned many valuable lessons, that would be wrong. God has surely given us the instinct of self-preservation because he has something for us to do in this life *which can only be learned in this life.* So we cling to it. It's instinctive. It's an innate urge to live and to continue to live as long as you healthily can.

Are you saying that this life is a preparation for a fuller life after death?

I think that is what it is for.

During your ministry, you must have been at the deathbed of many people. Would you feel there is any justification for having this terrible fear of death at the end, having seen people die?

I think there is no such justification. I have seen a number of people die, and I have made inquiries of nurses and doctors. You'll appreciate that most people die following a state of unconsciousness. Either they are in a coma or are drugged. But I have sat at the bedside of a man who was dying and conscious to the end. He gripped my hand, and I must have gripped his more tightly than I thought I was doing, for he said, "Don't hold me back, I can see through the gates. It's marvelous."

If you had seen, as I have, a woman so ill that she couldn't lift her head from the pillow, if you had seen her sit up, her eyes open with tremendous delight and joy in her face, if you had heard her call the name of her beloved husband, who had been dead twenty years, you would find it strangely convincing. People may say it was probably a hallucination, or a trick of the brain. All I can say is that it was very convincing to the onlooker that she really was in touch with the beloved dead and that he was coming back to welcome her.

I have collected dozens of incidents that point to our survival of death.

My own father-in-law spoke continually, when he was dying, of the presence of a daughter who had been dead for years. I remember also the case of a sister who was looking after a dying woman in one of our big teaching hospitals. The woman's son had committed suicide during the fatal illness of his mother, and therefore she was never told (I think his name was Michael). Yet she said to the sister, who told me about it, "Do you know, Michael has been with me all day today." Now, she did not know he had taken his life, so she was not imagining things, and I think that very likely he *was* near his mother.

Consider all these situations together and also remember that, at any rate in the inquiries I've made over a long period of years, never once has anybody died in mental unhappiness. They can show fear before the end; they can dread the idea of dying; but, if they are conscious to the last, the evidence is that it is an extremely happy experience. A physician to the royal family, when he was dying said, "If I had strength to hold a pen I would tell humankind what a wonderful thing it is to die."

In spite of this, most people mourn when they are separated from their loved ones by death. I think the Christian faith teaches us that this is mere selfishness and therefore sinful, and that wearing black for mourning is superstitious and dates back to ancient times. What would you say about that?

I wouldn't call it sinful. I think it's very natural for people who have loved someone very dearly to miss them terribly. You miss their physical presence, their voice, their eyes, their kiss, their radiant personality, their unhindered friendship.

But I would say two things about it. We ought to train ourselves to think something like this: "If this loved one of mine had gone to Australia I should be very sorry to miss him, but I should know that I should meet him again and that he was living and fulfilling a purpose and possibly doing something he had always wanted to do. No less is true if he has gone to the next life."

The second thing is that the evidence of those who have studied psychical research indicates that over-mourning, over-grief, and exaggerated sadness can hold the so-called dead back from entering into a happiness they would otherwise have. If we could say to ourselves, "I am terribly sorry and I feel very lonely, but I shall meet him again, and I want to rejoice in his freedom from disease and pain," I think then we should cheer ourselves up and we should probably do a service to the dead.

You have spoken of people dying in bed after a long illness and often in unconsciousness; but what about people who are knocked down in the street by a car or killed through other calamities? Do you feel they are equally prepared to die, and die as happily?

No. I think people who are knocked down and killed are certainly not prepared to die except insofar as their life and faith up to then have made them so. From the evidence of psychic research it seems that such people do not realize for some time that they are dead and it may take them a little time to realize that they are what is called "dead" and to adjust to another life. But that does not mean that entry into another world is unhappy or unpleasant for them. In all but the physical sense they go on where they left off.

Have you any examples to give of this?

I was thinking of examples like those Major Tudor Pole gives in one of his books (I think it is *The Silent Road*). He tells of a company commander who was shot early in a day's battle, but who was seen and heard by his men later to be still leading them on when presumably they did not know he was dead.

The same author tells of people who themselves did not know they were dead. I remember talking with a very distinguished man who told me of a friend of his who had allegedly come to him after his (the friend's) death. He said: "I was killed by a bus in the Strand, but I did not know I was dead. I went on to my office, and while I was there my partner said, 'I wonder what has happened to Sam, he's never late. What can have happened?' So I said to him, 'I'm here; don't worry; I am standing near you,' but he took no notice. Then I realized that there was something odd about the situation. Somebody else came—as it appeared to me, right through the wall—and said, 'Look, I'll explain things to you.' Then he said that I would gradually realize that I was what they called dead. But it took me a long time to realize this."

I believe that if one dies suddenly, like people who are shot or fall down a cliff or meet with an accident, it probably does take some time for them to realize that they are what is known as dead. But we mustn't surround the whole idea of dying with a melancholy atmosphere. They are still living;

there is no such thing as death regarded as the end. It is only moving from one room in the Father's house to another room.

Would you tell us in detail why we are here? What is the purpose of this life?

It's a complicated question. I think we are here as though we were children in a school who had things to learn in order to fit themselves for a further life beyond schooldays. Life on earth is comparable to one of the lower grades in God's school, and I think here we have to face certain problems, master certain temptations, and overcome certain difficulties in order to equip ourselves for a further life, which I take to be an increasing richness of communion with God.

Does this life decide our destiny for the next?

The fact of dying, in itself, does not seem to me to determine whether you go to hell or you go to heaven, although this is the view of certain Christian sects among us. I believe that when you die you go on where you left off. I can't believe that the accident of dying—which may be a drunken driver's mistake or the falling of coal into the pit or some other chance happening—determines our eternal destiny. Probably you would find that in the next phase that spiritual values seem more important. I hope it is so. You obviously leave behind you those demands which only the body makes, but the spiritual life seems more important and you long more and more to enter into it.

That's why it seems wise to try to look over our luggage and make sure that we are not carrying something that we won't be able to take past the "point of departure." I feel there may be an angel on the dock who looks at us and says, "Well, you won't want this and you won't want that—sex appeal, intellectual brilliance, social status, wealth." These things don't count for anything, surely. Not what I have done, but what I have become through my doing seems of immense importance. If I can develop humility and loving, and I would also add humor and a desire to serve others—these seem to me immensely important bits of luggage to carry. Is that the sort of thing you mean?

Yes. You are saying is that we are already spirit here and now, and that the way in which we lead our lives here does decide our destiny in the next life?

Yes, but it determines our destiny only in the same way that a man at the university who earns his degree determines the abilities that he can use when he follows his profession. But that does not mean that at death you remain forever what you are and cannot make any progress.

Could you explain what Jesus meant by "eternal life"?

I don't think he meant a life that merely goes on forever and ever and ever. That is to say, the quality of eternal life is not determined by length; it is determined by depth. Jesus meant by eternal life the life that the spirit of a person finds when it is in communion with God.

Some people seem to think that eternal life starts only when we die, but surely this isn't true?

No. The teaching of the Gospels, especially of the Fourth Gospel, is that eternal life is to be thought of as quality and not quantity—not in endless years but in a quality of communion with God that clearly begins now. You know, people say, "He's gone to be with God." But he has always been with God, and the highest heaven doesn't mean that God exists in any fuller measure. It can only mean that our power of communion deepens. But one of the marvelous things about the Christian gospel is that the offer of eternal life is here and now (John 5:24).

For example, where the first three Gospels use the phrase "enter the Kingdom of heaven" the Fourth Gospel speaks of "having eternal life." This goes to show that eternal life is a matter of the quality of one's living and not just going on forever and ever.

Can you describe this quality of life?
I feel that the Gospel writers mean life in harmony with God. Life always is correspondence with the relevant environment. The life of my eye is the ability to correspond with its relevant environment, which is light. The life of my ear ceases if its correspondence with sound ceases. Similarly the life of the soul is its correspondence with its relevant environment—which is God.

Does this mean that where there is no communion with God, eternal life is impossible? As I see it, a person can be alive here and have no communion with God, and yet she will have a soul nevertheless. Her soul will go on after she dies, after she lays down her physical body. But you have just now been saying that the life of the soul depends on communion with God—which this person has not had.

The answer is, I think, that there is no one who is entirely cut off from God. We are so apt to think of communing with God as something in terms only of religion. But there isn't any living soul, surely, in this world who is entirely blocked from the sense of beauty, from emotions roused by music, from love, from appreciation of various forms of art. In all these ways God is in touch with us. Communion with God isn't necessarily limited to prayer, going to church, and similar things, important though these are.

He who, for example, perceives beauty or shows compassion is in living communion with God even though it may be that he has not recognized it as such. It is inarticulate religion, but it's religion nonetheless.

But does such a person experience "eternal life"?

The way to it is always open to him. But he has not yet known it anything like as fully as he could do.

How can we help him know it better?

One way, I am sure, is to help him see that his appreciation of beauty, love, and also of truth is in fact an experience of God. If God is the author of these realities, then in a sense all who know them also know God.

CHAPTER 2

Is There Proof of Survival?

Dr. Weatherhead, many people find it very difficult to accept honestly in their own minds that there is a life after death, and yet human nature itself is evidence of immortality, isn't it?

Indeed it is.

Science has established surely beyond any reasonable doubt that humans have evolved out of nature and that they are raised above nature by their moral and spiritual ideals. Surely therefore it is unreasonable to believe that death is the end. You say in one of your books that if death were the end it would be as if the universe had produced its supreme creation and then flung it away like a capricious child throws away his or her toy. Could you enlarge on that idea? I am sure it would be helpful to many people.

I think that no one can arrive at death and say, "I have exhausted life's possibilities." In point of fact, few could claim even to have started to use their highest powers, such as the power to love, really to love. If there is no further plane on which those possibilities can be expressed, and if there is no opportunity to do the things of which we are capable, essentially capable by being human, then it seems to me that the whole of human life is irrational. Powers would have been created and then denied any expression.

But even if there is a universal belief that immortality is a fact, this does not necessarily make it a fact, does it?

No, it certainly doesn't. Yet in a rational universe, a universal longing seems to me to be a kind of signpost pointing in the direction of the satisfaction of the wish. If the world is a rational place, the fact that I feel hungry seems to me to point to the fact that there is such a thing as food. The terrific hunger of sex seems, in a rational world, to point to the fact that there is such a thing as a mate and the happiness of sexual fulfillment. Similarly the desire to go on after death at any rate points in the direction that it is likely. If you find ten signposts all pointing in a certain direction, it is fairly logical to suppose that there is a village there. Do you know what I mean?

I do. But on the other hand, our desire for sex and our desire for food are much stronger than our desire for the next world. In fact, we are most reluctant to go into the next world.

Well, *you're* reluctant because you're young. But I myself find that my desire to explore another world is far stronger, for instance, than my desire for food. And the idea that a desire for a particular thing is wishful thinking, and that that is an argument against the thing's existing, is a fallacy. If my beloved is terribly ill, I wish she would recover. That doesn't mean that she won't recover.

I think of a little boy separated from his family in the terrible days of World War II and being what they called an "evacuee," poor little kid. He dreamed literally night after night that he had a father and a family and love. This was wishful thinking, but it did not mean that there wasn't a family and a father and love. In the end, thank God, he was reunited with his family, and the reality was lovelier than the dream. In the same way, so many

25

thinkers have said that it's the passion to live again that makes us believe that we must live again, and the wishful thought is not a denial that it can be true. Wishful thinking does not mean that it is ridiculous.

No, but it doesn't prove it either.

No, it doesn't prove it. But in a rational world it makes it likely.

Then would you say there is any proof of life after death?

I regard it now as proved that humans live after death; that our consciousness is not just the result of chemical changes in the brain; that this consciousness does not perish when the brain dies; and that it has an individual existence, which, during our earthly life, has *used* the brain.

Somebody thought he was very, very clever when he said that our consciousness is like the light of the candle, and when the candle is used up the light goes out. This was alleged to be a proof that man's consciousness dies when the physical thing that gave it body, so to speak, perishes like the candle. But the very illustration is feeble, because the of the candle is still in the universe. If you had instruments fast enough and sensitive enough, you could recover that light. It's still vibrating through the universe after the candle itself is burnt out.

I see no reason to suppose that our consciousness, though it *uses* a brain, *dies* with that brain, any more than a person who is a violinist and expresses himself through his violin ceases to be a musician if you smash his violin. What's to stop him picking up another instrument and playing on that? When I die and this body rots in the grave and is absorbed into the matter of the universe, what is to stop my consciousness picking up some other instrument, such as an etheric body, and using that? You will find that this was Paul's idea in 1 Corinthians 15. Paul is very sound and modern in this when he says that God gives the soul another body in which it can express itself. The kernel of the wheat falls into the ground and dies, but we know that life springs up again in a different way.

Yes, and if this were not so, this planet of ours would surely be so overpopulated that we could just not cope with all the beings in it?
You mean, if we lived without dying? Yes, a terrible thought.

And so the "etheric" body takes up no room?

No, no. A spirit doesn't occupy space and an etheric body doesn't. While we are thinking about this theme, an analogy that appeals to me very much is one that came home to me when I was walking on the Scottish moors with my son and we found a lark's nest. In it were eggs ready to hatch. Within each egg was a bird with all the mechanism of eyes, ears, voice. Now, to say that death is our end seems to me as silly, as irrational, as stupid as to crush every egg before it hatches. Just as in that egg were latent abilities to sing, to see, to soar, so our abilities are not extinguished when we die. They are set free for further use. We have longings and yearnings and possibilities that can find their functioning only in a life beyond this. It makes sense of things, doesn't it?

CHAPTER 3

After Death: What Is It Like?

Could you give us any indication of what life might be like on the next plane?

I do really believe that Paul was making a right guess when he quoted, "Eye has not seen nor ear heard, neither have entered into the heart of man the things that God has prepared for them that love him" (1 Corinthians 2:9).

Would you say that we develop in life after death?

Oh, definitely. If there is life there must be growth. There can't be a thing called the static soul in another life any more than in this life. Either

29

you are going up or you are going down in this life and you remain "you"; and if somebody or something kills your body, that will not alter the fact that you are "you," and you will continue to go up or down.

Does this apply to those who do not die in faith as well as to those who do?

I confess that I am rather hesitant about this. I think it is terribly hard to assess the spiritual condition a person is in by such terms. The branch of the church that refers to "dying in faith" believes that at death your destiny is settled; that what you are at the point of death you are for all eternity. Some are going to be in heaven and some are going to be in hell. This I don't agree with at all, and I don't think it is true to the spirit and message of Jesus. A lot of people who deny the faith have never really had the faith fairly put to them. On the other hand a lot of people who profess a great deal and say they are "saved" don't impress me as having caught the spirit of Christ.

Then again, what are you going to do about all the people who haven't had any chance of understanding what Christ is talking about? What about the people of other faiths? Surely there is a way to God's heaven for the Buddhists and the Hindus and the Muslims. What are you going to do about little children who die before religion has any meaning at all? I can only suggest that at death we go on spiritually where we left off.

This then applies to the child who dies in infancy and has had no opportunity for soul growth; she goes on from where she left off?

Yes, and if you say she left off before she could have made any spiritual progress, surely there are helpers waiting for her on the other side. Nor do I exclude the idea that the child may come back again in some other life and find reality there, and take the exams, so to speak, which physical life demands from us.

Would you say that we sinners get a second chance?

Not only a second chance but a thousand chances. If the soul goes on where it left off and still has free will, it has power of choice. It can make the choice of climbing higher, or it can make the choice of indifference, or it can make the choice of descending lower. You can't have a free human spirit *compelled* to climb the higher way, can you?

No. Is the parable of Dives and Lazarus (Luke 16:19-31) relevant here?

I think it's relevant if you don't push it too far. It's rather dangerous to take any parable of Jesus, when it was spoken in a certain circumstance for certain people, and apply it to all circumstances and all people.

For instance, the parable of the rich young ruler could be quoted as though the possession of wealth was unchristian and unworthy. But Jesus was really saying to one man, "This is what is in the way of your spiritual progress." He cannot have meant to apply it to all such people, for Jesus himself depended on rich people, accepted the hospitality of rich men, and praised Abraham, who was one of the richest men in the Bible.

Now here is the parable of Dives and Lazarus. Dives is rich and feasting, and the poor beggar Lazarus is sitting in the road outside in rags, and also in pain and suffering. There were no serviettes and table napkins in those days, and the rich man uses pieces of bread to clean his fingers and then tosses them out of the window behind him. Lazarus, the poor beggar, picks them up and they become his only means of sustenance. Then, says

Jesus, they both die and pass into another world and the poor beggar is comforted and Dives is tormented. But he is not tormented by some outside devil. He is tormented by the insight that he now gains of what a selfish, thoughtless person he had been, and how inconsiderate he had been to others.

Now, in the parable Jesus says that the rich man pleaded with Abraham and said, "Do send somebody to tell my brothers lest 'they also come to this place of torment.'" In other words, "Do show them what I have now learned or else their consciences will torment them as mine is now tormented."

And Jesus has Abraham say, "It wouldn't be any good; they would not take any notice even if one rose from the dead." The parable seems to me to say that you can't thrust insight on a person. He has to go through experiences himself, which can be very painful (equals hell) until he himself discovers the truth about things. You asked if there is progress. Well, the rich man had already made progress because at least he became concerned about others. Before, he wasn't concerned about anybody except himself. He had no thought for his brothers, no thought for the beggar outside. The parable shows that at last, after death, he begins to think, "Oh dear, what about my poor brothers?" This is an advance, isn't it?

Yes, definite advance; and it is also comforting to learn that a child who died without having been given the opportunity to grow here also has the chance to advance there. Which leads me to wonder whether the mother, who must love this child, would meet her child again.

The answer is obviously yes, or it would be no heaven for the mother.

But then the child grows; the child does not remain a baby. Will the mother recognize her baby?

Yes, she certainly will. In the same way people say: "Look, my loved one died twenty years ago; he will have made immense progress in the spiritual world. If I die tomorrow, is he going to be so far advanced that we can't really join up together again? He will be so far ahead of me." But this is, in a way, "geographical" thinking, isn't it?

I tend to see things in pictures. I imagine a brilliant mathematician—let's imagine a professor in mathematics at Oxford, a person I knew. And let us imagine that he is sitting in his study, and at the table in his study his little boy is laboriously doing his sums. Now, there is an enormous gap between them; one is a professor of mathematics, the other is a child working out a simple addition sum. And you ask, *How can they have fellowship? He will never catch up with his father.* But their *love* relationship is not interfered with. Jesus said to the dying man on the cross, "Today you will be with me" (Luke 23:43). Well, there was an enormous gap between them in terms of spiritual advancement, but nevertheless Jesus promised that he would be with him. There is no gap in love, is there?

No. Love is probably the one essential; it bridges all gaps.

Exactly. I think it is important to reassure people of the reality of reunion, of the joy of it, of the amazing happiness of it, however they may differ in spiritual attainment. Those who love will delight in expressing their love by helping their loved ones.

This raises another problem—that of the person who has been happily married and one of the partners dies and the remaining partner marries again. Which of these two partners are they going to be happy with in the afterlife?

Well, yes, Jesus answered that. He said that in the resurrection there is neither marriage nor giving in marriage, but they "are as the angels" (Mark 12:25). I take that to mean that they are in quite a different relationship. A great part of the marriage union is the physical union, the physical attraction that one has for the other. Surely that fades out. I would think that we would be in a closer, even more loving relationship, devoid of sex and physical attraction, and a love-relationship that need not be restricted to one person.

This is what is so confusing. We are so possessive here with our love and think it is for us only and nobody else must have it. I think when we get over there we will understand love more fully, and will see that we can love many people.

Yes, but I would think that a husband and wife who have been very closely allied in spirit as well as body on this side have a special relationship. I don't see myself as being in exactly the same relationship to five hundred other women I have known as I am to my wife. Unless one of us repudiates it, I should think our lives will be entwined in a relationship of special closeness and increasing richness.

But that is possessive . . .

Not necessarily. The mere fact of marriage does not in itself mean union on the other side. Surely you are close only to those you love, and if a marriage has been only a semblance, if it has only been, "Oh, let's stick together for the children's sake"; if it has only been a convenient way of avoiding what the Joneses might think about a break-up, then I think it will provide no link, no power at all on the other side. There are of course far too many marriages based on that premise.

Exactly, and I find that there is far too little understanding of what love really is—think for example of 1 Corinthians 13—all of which will be given to us with greater understanding in the life after death. Dr. Weatherhead, could you enlarge a little more about what the next life is like?

Well, it's bound to be speculation, and Jesus himself was very reticent about it. Nobody knows of course what the "etheric" body is like, and what means of manifestation we have on the other side. I would agree with those who speculate that during this life we are weaving a sort of etheric counterpart, and that death simply means that we put down the physical part of our nature and continue our life in the etheric body. Now, that's a phrase that covers ignorance, and I can't pretend to dispel that ignorance very much. At first we might not realize we are dead, but after a time we might pass on to what is a more purely spiritual existence, but containing immense possibilities of enjoying beauty and of helping others.

But I think we have a glimpse of the quality of that life on this side of death. For instance, there are moments of tremendous spiritual exaltation, which I expect nearly everybody has had. Or think of a lonely person who suddenly finds herself truly loved and gives her love in return, and she feels secure and wanted and of supreme importance to somebody who seeks to share her life. Isn't that experience of being loved and having a chance fully to express love a foretaste of heaven?

Yes, I should think it probably is.

Some people find it in music. I am not educated in music enough to know, but some of my friends seem lifted, as they say, to a seventh heaven, by the works of the great masters. Wouldn't you think that was so? Wordsworth had a theory—I think he got it from Plato—which attracts me very much: that every beautiful thing you see on earth is a translation into matter of some unseen reality in the other world, in the world of spirit. When you look at a flower and admire its beauty, or when you listen to music and are thrilled by it, you are really getting a glimpse through the senses of a reality far greater and tremendously beautiful in the realm of spirit. I think that's an attractive idea.

Could one say that in such experience one is getting a view of God?

Yes, I think any experience of truth or beauty or goodness or love *is* an experience of God.

Dr. Weatherhead, we are constantly impressing on people that we are here not only as physical bodies, but that we have a mind and we have a spirit. We know the necessity for them to feed their spirits and cultivate their spiritual life in order to live a decent life and to build character. Now I think many of them might be confused when we also bring in concepts like "soul" and "essential personality," which go on after we have put down these physical frames of ours. Could you say something to make that clear?

I will do the best I can. My own vision is so limited that it's a bit difficult. I would equate soul and spirit. I would say that humans are a trinity in unity—we are body, mind, and spirit. Now the body clearly is that physical part of ourselves through which we make contact with the outside world. The mind is that unseen, immaterial part by which we express thoughts. We have mind in common with the animals, although ours is much more developed; and whereas the animal knows, we *know* that we knows. We are self-conscious personalities. Now the brain is to be remembered as part of the body. I use my brain to think as I use my hands to feel, and the fact that when I die, my body, including my brain, falls into dust doesn't mean that my mind stops existing—as I mentioned earlier—any more than when a violinist smashes his violin he ceases to be a musician. He could go and pick up another instrument and play it. And I believe that I survive death, but instead of having a brain with which to think and communicate, I have some other kind of instrument that is suitable to my new environment.

Now the spirit (the soul and spirit I take to be the same) I regard as that part of the mind with which I can worship, that part of my immaterial being that is capable of communion with God. That's how I distinguish body, mind, and spirit. When one talks about the "essential personality," this is what I believe survives. I mean that immaterial part of myself that is the real "me."

It has *used* a body, it has *used* a brain, but it is essentially mind-spirit.

Yes, I think that has made it somewhat clearer. But there is still another complication because we bring in this term "etheric" body. So am I right, then, in thinking that the mind and spirit and essential personality are all one with the etheric body?

Yes, I speculate that, just as in this world we need a body with which to express ourselves, when we pass into the next sphere of being, there must be some means of manifestation, which I call the etheric body. Otherwise I would not be able to communicate with my loved ones, I would not be able to have fellowship with others, I would not be able to serve others; and there must be some means (which I call the etheric body) by which

41

I recognize my friends in another world and am recognized by them, and differentiated from other spirits.

You see, if any existing animal knew only two dimensions—say length and breadth—then something that also had height would be unperceivable by that animal because it would be manifested in a dimension foreign to itself. May it not be that when we pass into another life there are other dimensions in which being can be manifested—so that what is impossible for us to see and register by the senses we now have, would be perceptible in a life in which there was another dimension.

To sum up, there must be some form of manifestation after we have finished with this body by which we can express ourselves, and through which we can be recognized.

Yes. Would an etheric body be a right term to use when referring to the resurrection of the body of Jesus?

I should think so. It was evidently a body manifesting itself in a very different way from our own—perceptible to some, imperceptible to others; able to pass through closed doors; able to travel great distances. I think it would be quite fair to call it an etheric body, though in a sense that phrase is only a label for us to use in our ignorance.

So to recap, on this plane we have the physical body that can suffer physical illnesses and have physical sensations; we have a mind with which we can think and we can also have mental illnesses. So we have a physician to treat the physical body, a physician specialized in psychiatry to treat the mind, and a minister to treat the soul.

This is ideal, yes, if they all know their jobs! And ideally if they cooperate as a team.

But even in this life the different parts of our personalities are all interwoven, aren't they, and they can't be separated one from another really, and shouldn't be separated in treatment?

Oh, I entirely agree, and this was taught by Plato years before Christ. You must deal with the *whole* person, he said, including the soul. The soul can be sick and make the body and mind sick, just as much as the body and mind can be sick from physical causes alone.

Dr. Weatherhead, there is a widespread fear that

people who die mentally sick go into the next life mentally ill. This isn't true, is it?

No, I am sure it isn't. For one thing, a great deal of mental illness is due to physical causes so that when you lay down the physical body, you know you have finished with that. But the kind of illustration that I like to use is to think of a mentally ill patient as a person sitting in a room with the kind of crinkly glass in the windows that is used for bathrooms and such. Let's suppose he is locked in and can't get out. When he looks out on the world he sees a distorted world, and when people look at him through the window they see a distorted person. But it's the glass, not the person, and when the house of life is left, the person walks out as himself. That is to say, the essential personality is untouched, whether the illness was caused physically or through distorted emotional conflicts.

Would you say that we shall be able to recognize people we have known only by repute, people of earlier generations, and so forth?

Well, of course, I don't know. The main evidence in the New Testament is that Jesus is said to have had communion with Moses and Elijah on the mount of transfiguration (Matthew 17: 1-8). So he seemed to be able to come into contact with people of earlier generations. I would imagine that it is possible. But I think that there must be some link other than mere curiosity to see what the great are like and so on. Wouldn't you think that there must be some linking of souls, in the same way as we speak of "kindred spirits"? I think there must be. It's difficult to understand exactly what happens, but if two persons are sufficiently attracted to each other, the length of time that one person has been in the next world should not necessarily deter them from meeting.

Will time, as we now understand it, have any part in the afterlife?

I find that a very difficult question, because for the life of me I cannot imagine a timeless existence any more than I can imagine a spaceless existence. It may well be that time in the life after death has not the same relationship to us as it has now. That is to say, we may have equal access to the past, present, and even the future. But inasmuch as I am now alive on this earth and at some point in time

45

will pass through into another phase of existence, there must be a difference, surely, to those on the other side between the "now" to me and the "now" to them. I mean there must be some point at which I enter their world, and it must be a point in time, as I now understand time, surely.

Yes, but not time as we now understand it, because time as we now understand it is in some ways a human invention.

Humans gave the day its twenty-four hours because of the rising and the setting of the sun, and then grouped the days into weeks and the weeks into months and the months to form a year. I don't think time in that way will apply in the next life as far as I can imagine it.

You mean that in the next life you will not say, "I will meet you next Thursday afternoon"? And yet I can't myself imagine any phase of existence where time has no meaning at all. For example, there must come a time (to use the word) when God's plan for humanity is completed.

Yes, don't you think space is similar? Space must be something very different in the next world from what we know it to be here. One imagines and speculates that the spirit does not occupy space, so that an etheric body is independent of space as we know it.

Dr. Weatherhead, what part, if any, does memory of events in this life play in the life after death?

Well, remember the parable of Dives and Lazarus and how Abraham says to Dives, "Son, remember that you in your lifetime received your good things and Lazarus in like manner evil things" and now the situation is reversed, or words to that effect (Luke 16:25). Apparently, if we are not claiming too much from the language used, memory does go on, and one would imagine that part of one's purgatory is to remember with regret the things that one has done that are wrong. I would also think that part of one's purgatory is to suffer with any person one had wronged until that person forgave one and thus purged the evil that had been wrought. I am rather afraid that memory *will* go on and it will be very painful to remember some things, just as it will be heaven to remember some other things, like the experience of loving, serving, and the enjoyment one had in beauty. Do you remember the poem by Bishop Stubbs?

I sat alone with my Conscience
    In a place where time had ceased.
We discoursed of my former living
    In a land where the years increased,
And I felt I should have to answer
    The questions it put to me,
And to face those questions and answers
    In that dim eternity.
And the ghosts of forgotten actions
    Came floating before my sight,
And the sins that I thought were dead sins
    Were alive with a terrible might.
And I know of the future Judgment,
    How dreadful so e'er it be,
That to sit alone with my conscience
    Would be judgment enough for me!

That says rather a lot, doesn't it?

Yes. It emphasizes that the memory of sin committed in this world may torture you in the next. But surely if one has repented of one's sins here and accepted forgiveness, these are obliterated and cease to disturb one?

Yes, I think this is a very important point, and

I am so glad you raised it. Forgiveness restores relationship, and there is plenty of evidence of that in the Bible. "I will forgive their iniquity and their sin will I remember no more" (Jeremiah 31:34). "As far as the east is from the west, so far hath he removed our transgressions from us" (Psalm 103:12).

At the same time, as I try to meditate on the point, I feel that in the next phase of being, if clearer light on sin is granted to me, I shall still be bitterly ashamed that I ever hurt my loving Father by doing the things that I did. And although penalty is obliterated—the penalty of sin being separation from God—although I am one with him, surely I shall still deeply regret that I ever did what I did and bear scars that can't be completely eradicated. Forgiveness does not obliterate consequences, though it alters them from resented pain to accepted discipline.

Do you know what I mean? The prodigal comes home again, and the relationship is restored. At once he is a son; he is back at home. But surely he still bears the scars of his adventures, perhaps in his body but certainly in his mind and his spirit, and thinks, "However did I come to hurt my father like that?" Wouldn't that become the source of new energy to serve with greater devotion? God can make of *forgiven* sin a qualification and asset with which one can help others similarly tempted.

Yes. Do you think that is why without the father having to say a word—no condemnation, no inquiry—the prodigal just knew that he was forgiven and accepted?

Yes, this is so. Judgment to me is never the judgment imposed by a judge on a throne who tells a trembling sinner that he is hell-bound. Judgment to me, in the realm of religion, means judgment we pass on ourselves in the light of Christ's love and God's long-suffering in giving mercy.

In the life after death has sin any place at all?

Here again I am speculating. I can't understand how the accident of death, as it often is, can make one incapable of sinning. If one has free will and choice, surely there must be a measure of temptation, the overcoming of which is the basis of one's growth. I can understand that as one grows spiritually and understands more of what God's nature is, and what his love involves, one is less and less tempted. I can't understand how a person, until he or she really achieves perfection and unity with God, can be automatically made sinless by the accident of dying. And although, having lost one's body one isn't tempted to certain types of sin, and since one is not in possession of any material thing there is no temptation to steal, I would think that there could still be a temptation to pride or jealousy or envy or resentment or even hate.

CHAPTER 4

How Can We Prepare Ourselves?

Can you tell us how we can best prepare ourselves for the next life? We seem to be more occupied in making ourselves comfortable in this one. This seems to be our main concern—getting all the pleasures we can out of this life, mainly physical pleasures. How then can we best prepare ourselves for the next?

This is where Christ's coming into our lowly flesh has tremendous importance. The final goal of life after death is to be one with God, to be fitted to share his amazing, glorious life. Then the sooner we give up concentrating on values such as you have hinted at—being comfortable, squeezing the last drop of pleasure out of life for ourselves, attaining high rank and important positions—the sooner we see that it is more important to develop character, develop capacity for God, the better it will be for us.

We are so often the victims of a faulty sense of values. Archbishop Temple once said it is as though somebody got into a shop in the night and altered the price labels of the things in the shop, so that valuable things were marked low, and useless things were marked high. Now that is exactly what has happened in this life. Things like obligation, service to others, a sense of duty, unselfish sacrifice, humility—these things are marked low. But having a good time, gaining your ends socially, sexually, materially, academically— these are marked high. This is one of the things that is wrong with the world. It's living as though there were nothing else after death, and this is wrong or—to say the least—mistaken. Belief in survival helps us get our sense of values right.

Humanity has been on earth a very long time and doesn't seem to be making very much progress in soul growth.

No. And yet think of the days when a man was hanged for stealing a dollar; think of the days when boys of thirteen were working in the mines for twelve, thirteen, and fourteen hours a day; think how a person was fired ruthlessly and left without any unemployment benefit or state aid because he displeased a tyrannical boss. We have made progress in things like these. Think of the days of slavery, when slaves were the property of the owners; and men could rape the female slaves and beat a slave to death. From that kind of ruthless cruelty and barbarity there has been tremendous progress in the modern period.

But not on the same scale as progress in physical and scientific spheres.
No, I'm afraid not.

But if we are now already spirits, or souls, whatever the term is, what do we do that hinders our soul's growth?
Surely what would hinder our soul's growth would be a concentration on things that have no significance after death. I mean if I put all my energies into getting rich, if I put all my energies into academic accomplishments, if I put them all into attaining social status, into being a little bit better than the Joneses, this is no kind of preparation for the next world.

But if, on the other hand, I put my emphasis into trying to serve other people, comforting the distressed, helping the troubled, working for the good of all humankind and so on—serving my fellows—that is giving me better qualifications for the next world.

Could you enlarge on what happens to our souls if we don't feed them?

Surely the answer is that we shall enter the other life, where spiritual values are more clearly seen to be important, like a teacher, shall we say, who wants to teach but fails his degrees. We shall be in an inferior condition to function in the next world, but we may still be allowed to go on making progress and forsake the false ideals of our earlier life. Or we may indeed—and this is only an opinion (but it is shared by about five hundred million other people, all the Hindus and Buddhists)—be allowed to come back and take the "exams" again in another incarnation. I find nothing in this idea to conflict with the Christian faith, and I find a lot in it that makes sense of some of the anomalies and apparent injustices of this life.

Yes, but I don't want at this stage to go into reincarnation. I am rather more concerned with the encouragement of soul growth and what happens if we neglect the soul. You have used analogies in the past of what would happen to our physical bodies if we were to neglect any part of them. For example, if we were blindfolded for long periods our eyes could become useless. Is this applicable as well to our souls?

Yes, I think so. Just as eyes need light, just as the lungs need air, just as the ears need sound, just as the mind needs truth, so the spirit or the soul needs communion with God. Because the eyes need light, because light is the only environment in which they can function, if light is cut off they atrophy, and the same is true in the other cases I have hinted at. If you cut yourself off altogether from God and things spiritual, your soul diminishes in its power to live, so that if you are thrust suddenly by death into a spiritual world you are like a half-blind person confronted with a sunset. Or I would say you are a like tone-deaf person who finds he is in a marvelous concert that other people, who have developed their musical faculties and their hearing, can appreciate, but it is boring and meaningless to him.

Can you think of any other illustrations of things that might hinder soul growth? For example, if I give way to certain temptations, whether just bad temper or sexual desire, and can say to myself, "Well, I think I won't count this time; it doesn't matter this time," does this have any effect?

Surely it does. Somebody once said, "God will forgive you, but your nervous system won't." That is to say, if you plunge into, say, sexual extravagances, increasing physical desire, and then you pass over into a world where the physical does not exist, you have increased something that cannot function there, to the detriment of your spirit. But if you strengthen the spirit by prayer, by meditation, and by loving others, you increase your capacity to enjoy life. Does that seem clear?

Yes, but I would like some more examples.

Let me put it this way. Two people go to a concert. One is a musician to his fingertips; he has studied music, he loves music; great music played by great artists is heaven to him. He sits next to a person who is tone deaf, to whom music means nothing, and who sits there just wishing for the intermission when he can have a drink, something that he can enjoy. Now, they are sitting next to each other, but between them there is a great gulf fixed. Jesus talked about a great gulf being fixed (Luke 16:26). It may not be fixed forever, but it is fixed for the time being, inasmuch as the musician cannot inject his friend with the love of music. His friend, supposing the concert went on forever, could begin to be taught how to enjoy music. Now this, to me, is the difference between heaven and hell. Surely, heaven to the spiritual person is like a good concert to the musical person; she feels, This is where I belong, this is marvelous, this is life to me. Hell, surely, is to be in a situation where one is bored and there is nothing left to enjoy, and where one suffers remorse at one's own shortsightedness.

I would like to come back to what you have just been saying, because I am sure there is great value in the idea that you have given about the two friends going to a concert, one being able to appreciate the music and one not being able to. But while we are considering factors that might harm soul growth, can you think of any other illustrations?

There is one that comes to my mind, which I have quoted before, concerning putting off till tomorrow or some later date the determination to put right in ourselves what we know to be wrong. I can remember meeting a man with whom I struck up a conversation about poetry. Our host was a very charming, generous, and lovable man, but his life was mainly given up to making his business a success. Overhearing us he said, "You know, when I retire I am going to take up poetry."

Now, you cannot do that. You cannot deny a culture like poetry, music, or art until you are about seventy and say, "Go to, I will now enjoy poetry." And it is highly dangerous to say, "Well, I am going to have a right good time here, I am going to give way to all my instincts, I am going to make money and enjoy myself thoroughly on the physical plane; and when I see death looming up, I will switch over to spiritual things." Of course it is better to switch over than not to do so, but we must not expect to catch up at once with the man who has been a lifelong saint.

So it is essential to direct our thoughts as early as possible to spiritual things and to be concerned by spiritual problems. Now, how best can we do this?

You know as well as I do all the devotional aids,

like prayer, meditation, the Bible, good literature, corporate worship, and Christian fellowship. I would very much like also to get in a word here that there are many things in life that are religious that are not labeled religious. I object to the idea that saying prayers, going to church, and reading the Bible are necessarily more spiritually enriching than, say, a great concert, great poetry, or the love of nature. God fulfills himself in many ways. Anything that makes the spirit of man respond to beauty or truth or love or goodness is enriching to his soul, and through these things he can increase his spiritual stature.

I said I would revert to the analogy of the two friends going to a concert, one being able to appreciate good music and the other not. I think there may be some danger in laboring appreciation of the arts, because am I not right in thinking that there are other things of the spirit—a relationship with Christ, for example, or a relationship with a good person— that can do a bad person a lot of good? Have you anything to say on that?

Yes. Clearly the whole heart of Christianity is a relationship with the living Christ. The very word "religion" means "a link," the ligament, the thing that binds you to something else, and it is this relationship which is nourished by prayer and religious meditation and so on.

Would you not say that this is the number one essential for spiritual growth?

Yes, I was using the concert only as an illustration. The person who loves Christ starts in the next world with an enormous advantage over the one to whom Christ is a meaningless word. People noticed in the disciples a transformation, and they attributed it to the fact that they had been with Christ (Acts 4:13). This we should all endeavor to do during our daily lives. The more time we can spend in a conscious relationship with Christ the better we become.

Can you give us some more illustrations of what would help us grow spiritually, since this is the only thing that really matters in life?

Yes, but there is a danger in separating secular and sacred and saying, "I grow more, spiritually, by meditation and thinking about Christ than in doing my daily work." There is a catch here. It may be the calling, the vocation, of some people to be monks or to be nuns, but Jesus never made this kind of distinction between sacred and secular. I think a thing is made secular not by what it is but by the way you do it. Runing a home so that all the wheels run smoothly and you do not hear them grinding; spending one's life ministering to people within that home; serving other people's needs, as you do—these are as sacred, it seems to me, in the eyes of Christ, as giving people Holy Communion or preaching sermons.

I am not quite sure that that is what I meant. I am recalling what Edward Wilson once wrote to the effect that if we were to give as much time to our spiritual well-being as we give to our physical well-being, humankind would make terrific strides forward. He gives the illustration that we get up in the morning and bathe and feed and clothe ourselves, and look after the comforts of physical well-being, but a vast majority of us have no concern at all for spiritual well-being.

Yes, indeed. I am sure we ought to spend more time in spiritual culture. But you can see my own argument if you take it to an extreme. Here is a man who sits in his study, let us say, and declares,

"I will spend today in spiritual culture for my own soul," and by so doing rejects an invitation to go and help someone who is bereaved, or says "No" to a person who says, "I am ill; will you come and see me?"

I couldn't agree with you more. It seems to me we are out of balance. We are giving far too much time to our physical well-being and far too little to our spiritual, and our spiritual well-being must include service to others.

We are often asked if it is morbid to think about death. My answer would be, "Of course not." Natural death is as normal as birth. Both are within God's plan. I think it is essential for their soul growth and personality that young people should think about death. Death is a mystery; life is a mystery; life on earth is full of mystery. Plant life, animal life, every wave of the ocean, every star that shines—each has its own hidden mystery. Life hereafter is also a mystery, God's mystery, full of blessings. Why then should people be turned away from the greatest and best of all mysteries? Why should people not seriously contemplate the incomparably great and unseen life that lies before them and into which they must inevitably embark someday? There is nothing morbid in that. It would only be morbid and unwholesome if they thought that death was the end, but it is not. Do you agree with me?

Well, in part. I think it would be morbid if young people full of life and bursting with energy and happiness—loving and being loved, for instance—continually allowed their minds to dwell on death. I think that would be morbid. I can only go back to my own experience. I am sure that as a teenager and a young man I didn't let my mind dwell on death. I think, however, that from time to time it is a good thing if people are challenged with the fact that one must die sometime.

A very dear friend of mine was in an office that was bombed in the war and everybody was killed except herself. She was covered with other people's blood and had a very terrible experience. She said to me, "On that day I decided that I would always try to live each day as if it were my last." Now that was not morbid. I think the whole idea that death was very near but did not touch her has influenced her for good. From time to time it's a very good thing if all of us come to terms with the idea of death, rob it of its terrors, think our way through the problem, and so on. As you say, it is as natural as birth. But to be quite honest and down to earth, I would think that a teenager, healthy and full of life, would be morbid if she let her mind continually dwell on death.

CHAPTER 5

What If We Are Not Christians?

Some things that Jesus said about life after death can be understood by most people. But what about phrases like "I am the bread of life and if any man eat of this bread he shall live for ever" (John 6:51)? Suppose a person were not a Christian, but a Jew or a Hindu, and did not understand. What happens to such people? They need a life after death, too, don't they?

Yes, of course. I think the only answer I can give is, I don't know what happens to them. I am sure that life after death contains further choices, further visions, of what is ultimately desirable, so that Jews, Muslims, Buddhists, and Hindus find everything that was true in their religion justified. But I also believe that they find Christ to be someone who can reveal even more to them, so that they don't have to deny anything that was true in their religion, and yet find Christ offering further insight and understanding of what communion with God means. It is like a person climbing the foothills of the Himalayas and then finding the shining heights still beyond him. With the vision will come a burning desire to climb still higher. Christ is the summit of the Hindu road as he is of the Christian way. I do not believe that because a person has not been a Christian she perishes at death, if that is what you mean. I won't believe that for a moment.

Yet this seems to be what the words of Christ imply, but they are probably misunderstood. "I am the bread of life and if any man eat of this bread he shall live for ever" seems rather to rule out the others. Do people of other faiths believe in life after death?

Indeed they do.

Of all other faiths?

As far as I know, they do. Muslims believe that they will be welcomed into paradise and have a wonderful life there; Hindus believe that they will come back and be incarnated in other and presumably higher forms of life. I do not know any religion that asserts that we are finished by the accident of dying. This would seem to me absolutely irrational.

In your opinion, Dr. Weatherhead, will all be won for God in the end?

Well, there are people in various churches who would deny what I believe. They think that death does determine what happens to you and that the righteous go into what they call everlasting life, and that the wicked go into hell, I suppose. Now I can't understand this, and I am not just speculating without any basis. Paul says, God "willeth that all should be saved and come to the knowledge of the truth" (1 Timothy 2:4). A greater authority still, Jesus, when he gives us the parables of the lost sheep and the lost coin and the lost son (Luke 15), uses in two of those stories the words "until he find it." The shepherd goes over the mountain and looks for the sheep "until he find it"; the woman looks for the coin "until she finds it"; the ever-loving father is unhappy about the prodigal until he comes home. "As in Adam all die," says Paul, "so in Christ shall all be made alive" (1 Corinthians 15:22).

Now I don't see how God, who is Love, can be satisfied if there is one soul in an endless hell, if there is one soul lost. That is a defeat of eternal purpose; and that, I don't believe, is possible. I don't know how many phases of life on the other side of death are involved or how long it will take or what will happen. But I can't believe that even any human person capable of love can be in perfect bliss if there is one soul in endless unhappiness and grief and pain. How much less can God be content? So I don't think there will be heaven— not the highest heaven—for anybody, least of all for God, unless we are all in it.

Can a Christian wife hope to meet her husband who has died having made no profession of faith at all, and perhaps having denied having any faith?

I think the answer must be that if she loves her husband and her husband loves her, they will be reunited and have fellowship together. One must not suppose that the life after death is, so to speak, all within the field of religion, as we understand it, any more than this life is.

You see, people recognize that this life is a tremendously complex system of communication with other people who by and large have no reference to religion at all. I do not see why we should regard life after death only in a religious context. I think religion is equally and even more important, but I think some people imagine that the next world will be like attendance at one very long service in a church. I should hate that and so would you.

It's quite indisputable that we are all going to die, and to my way of thinking we are all going to live again in the next world, whether we are members of any church or any faith or no faith.

I think so, too.

What about people who never attain to communion with God at all?

If the soul was cut off entirely from any contact with God, the logic of the situation would be that the soul would die. Science, at any rate, knows nothing of an organism that is permanently cut off from its environment and yet goes on living.

But I would have thought that even those people who have repudiated religion as we understand and have experienced it are nevertheless able to come into touch with God. Every time they admire a sunset they are in communion with God; every time they serve a neighbor they are in communion with God; every time they respond to the love of a child they are in communion with God.

I think we have got to be very careful not to limit communion with God to the framework provided by religion. Bernard Shaw said, "There is as much healing power in a Beethoven sonata or a painting by Constable as there is in some excerpts from the Bible." I believe this is true, and I am sure that many a devoted Christian thinks that if he reads a psalm through at night, this is a religious activity, but that if he listens receptively to beautiful music, that is not a religious thing to do. Surely this distinction is false. I think we agree that any sensitive contact with beauty, truth, love, or goodness is an experience of God.

CHAPTER 6

At the Very End

Dr. Weatherhead, as I understand some religious teachers, they speak about a final judgment. Could you comment and explain that to some degree?

I don't think that there is such a thing as a final judgment. If a spirit remains free, this means that he's always free to choose, and to say that any choice must be his final choice seems to me a contradiction of that freedom. My own view is that God wills that every living soul shall at last be by free choice into harmony with his will. I understand that it may be aeons of time, as we think of time, before everyone is brought in. But the Bible seems to be very strong on this point that all shall be saved and come to a knowledge of the truth. So I believe that finally, without any coercion or any unfair use of force, the soul will come to see that its highest welfare is in saying yes to God. And that finally this will happen and all created beings will be brought into harmony with God, in an ultimate heaven the nature of which we simply haven't the power to imagine.

Is it right to assume that at death humans wish to pursue their highest ideals? And if not, is this the difference between heaven and hell?

I think it is. On the one hand, a good person with ideals that she wishes to realize finds herself in a sphere in which she can more and more ably express those ideals. But a person who at death has no great desire to express his highest nature may find himself in the very strange and painful situation in which the only things he can do are those he has no desire to do. This, it seems to me, illustrates very well the central difference between heaven and hell.

But this is not necessarily his final state?

I do not see why it should be. The person who is thoroughly bored with music, for example, can begin to learn music. So surely death doesn't determine our final destiny. Surely a person in another world—let's take this illustration of music—where he finds music is the great reality and the source of joy begins (a) to wish that he had paid more attention to it earlier, and (b) to listen to it and study it so that he can appreciate it.

As for judgment, I never think of this as a great white throne where God says to one person, "You are for everlasting life" and to another, "You are to be in an endless hell." Judgment is passed upon us by the nature of the sphere in which we find ourselves. Let's look again at the analogy of the concert. The two men who go to the concert are judged by the music. Nobody comes onstage and says, "You're no good because you can't appreciate it, and you are marvelous because you can." The music itself judges the person by whether he is at home with it or bored by it.

This is what Jesus meant when he said he did not to judge the world but to save the world (John 12:47). Then, according to the Fourth Gospel, he added, "The word that I spake, the same shall judge him in the last day" (v. 48). To me, every day, in a sense, is a judgment day. When beauty or truth or goodness or love confront you, and you love them and respond to them and accept them and would like to develop them, then you are judged as a lover of these things. If they bore you or you think they are valueless, then they condemn you.

Dr. Weatherhead, when you were talking about a final judgment, you said that a soul is free and has the power of choice. But does there ever come a time when finally there is no choice left to us?

I can't conceive that there can ever be a time when a spirit with free will is doomed and has no further chance of finding God. For one thing it would be a divine failure. If one single soul loved by God, as well as loved by other people, passed into nothingness, this would be a divine defeat.

I think that there can never come a time when a soul cannot turn to God and begin to live more fully. I suppose theoretically we have to say that the soul could go on saying no to God. But I cannot bring myself to believe that that can ever be final because, as I say, that is a defeat for God and it is the loss of a precious soul, and it denies free will, one of the essential qualities of the soul. Although you can say, theoretically, that a person could always choose darkness, darkness, darkness, darkness and never choose light, surely as she goes through all the training in God's further schools for the soul after this life, she will be brought to the point where she longs for the light and will respond to God. Maybe she had never before seen light as beautiful and desirable.

Yes, and that person will gradually come out of the pitch darkness into gray and then another shade of darkness until she must eventually progress forward. Not necessarily quickly, but God has plenty of time.

You see, we talk about a defeat of God. But surely there cannot be heaven for anybody if one soul is debarred from entering it. This is so even if it is that soul's own fault. If a person is run over in the street and it is entirely his own fault, you don't refuse to take him to the hospital so he can be treated. In the infinitely more crucial situation of a soul's eternal welfare, the same principle must surely apply. However much the fault is ours, and in greater or less measure it always is, the love of God will never cease to try to win us.

So this means that no choice a soul makes will in fact prove final because God himself will not accept it as final?

No, because God himself will not accept it as final.

CPSIA information can be obtained at www.ICGtesting.com
Printed in the USA
BVOW06s2307220916

462699BV00026B/52/P